Let's Build a Playground

How deep? How heavy? How many? How long? Measurements are everywhere when you build a playground. But big numbers are often hard to picture. So let us help! Whenever a big number comes along, just think of me and my friends. We're the size of many kids in kindergarten. We each weigh about 40 pounds and we're about 40 inches tall. And when we stretch our arms wide, they span 40 inches, too. So I'll tell you how many of me and my friends it would take to make up a number.

Let's Build a Playground

A  Book

MICHAEL J. ROSEN

PHOTOGRAPHS BY

ELLEN KELSON
AND
JENNIFER CECIL

CANDLEWICK PRESS

What if, one day, you built a playground

right where there wasn't one before —

where kids had no place to play?

Lucky us! Our school joined with **KaBOOM!,** an organization that believes kids everywhere need a fun, nearby place to exercise their bodies and their imaginations. They've already helped more than 2,200 communities across North America come together to create playspaces of their own.

3

What if you built a brand-new playground
    right where a rickety, rusty one stood —
        in a place where no one wanted to play?

What if, one day, the whole community
    built a playground where everyone
        could swing and climb and jump and slide and bounce . . .

a playground where anyone could conjure
    a game or a silly sport right on the spot,
        or pretend to be a racer, wrestler, or dancer?

One day — *KaBOOM!* — we did!
    We built a playground in our neighborhood!
        How did we build it? *KaBOOM!*
            How can you build it? *KaBOOM!*

First step: everyone joined in —
    parents and neighbors, grandparents and teachers,
    kindergartners and eighth-graders
    and every grade in between.
        We all met with the team from KaBOOM!

So what's your dream playground? they asked us all.
    And sure, we had ideas! So many, we drew pictures
    to share them with one another.
        And then we voted so that our playground
        would truly be our very own.

Let's have a bounce house!
   A dinosaur dig with real fossils!
      A merry-go-round!

How about a train and a submarine to pilot?
   A hot tub. A tower. How about a roller coaster
      that transforms into a rocket?

We need a spiraling slide!
   A lemonade stand!
      A sand castle — big enough to hide inside!

We got to choose our playground's colors, too!
   We picked the perkiest green — just like spring!
      And the sunniest yellow — just like summer!
         We made so many suggestions that we had to vote
            on the third color. Purple — like plums — won!

Building a playground takes so much planning!
The grown-ups divided into groups.
We'll recruit more volunteers!
We'll take care of all the safety plans.
Let us organize breakfast and lunch
for the day we assemble the playground.
Okay, we'll stake out the boundaries
and bring a bulldozer to prepare the site.

We kids, we contributed, too.
To help raise money, we challenged
the teachers to a basketball game
and charged admission.
(We tried! But the teachers won. . . .)
We held a car wash. We hosted a dance.

And we cooked up a project of our own:
we painted dozens of stepping stones
for the entrance to our playground.

Two sides of our playground are 50 feet long. The other sides are 70 feet long. It takes 72 of us, stretching out our arms and touching hands, to surround the giant rectangle. If we invited all our friends to stand shoulder to shoulder, 3,500 of us could squish inside our playground.

A **Bobcat** is a type of compact track loader: a smaller vehicle that moves on tracks like a bulldozer and can glide over rough or muddy ground. It has a loader—a blade, bucket, or other tool—that can move dirt and other materials. But not just a little: It can lift 3,000 pounds! That's like me and 74 friends . . . *if* we could all fit inside the shoveling blade!

When we built our playground,

I wanted to be the person who drove the bulldozer.
Its scooping blade scraped the ground to brown
and heaved the heavy sod to the side.
A dozer is like a grazing dinosaur!
A munching dino-dozer!

When I drew my dream playground,
it had an enormous apatosaurus to slide down!
From his head, you could glide along his neck,
zoom across his back, swoop around his tail —
and race back up for another ride!

When you draw **your** playground,
what will you dream up?

A zooming submarine that
sneaks under the waves?

A wizard's castle with a winding
staircase to spiral down?

An icy hillside for tobogganing
onto a frozen lake?

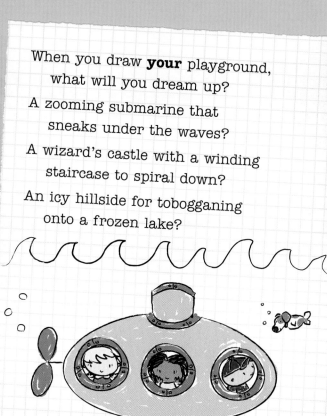

When we built our playground,

I wanted to drive the colossal semi-trailer
that hauled and dumped the chopped-up trees
that were chunked and chipped into bits.

When I drew my dream playground,
I made a mountain as tall as Mount Everest —
it's in the Himalaya Mountains! —
with a fortress at the snowiest peak.

It's tough work trekking up the steep slopes,
but once I'm at the tippy top —
higher than falcons soar, higher than rainbows float —
I sled the whole way down without a stop!

For our playground . . .
a huge truck drove onto
the blacktop and dumped
out a mountain of mulch!
Fifty-three tons—106,000
pounds—of chopped-up
wood. That weighed as
much as 2,650 of us kids!

When you draw **your** playground,
will there be a pirate ship
whose mast you'll climb
into the pillowy clouds?

A magic ladder that leads to
an ogre's sky-high lair?

A castle wall to scramble over
so you escape a wizard's spell?

A **skid steer** is a one-person vehicle with mechanical arms that attach to a bucket, blade, backhoe, or fork. On construction sites, it can lift, dig, and haul. Why is it called a skid steer? The wheels on one side move independently of the wheels on the other side. So it can skid or pivot in place when the driver needs to steer it into tight spaces.

When we built our playground,

I wanted to be the one who operated the skid steer
with the auger — that monster drill that spirals
into the ground, boring down and down,
to bring up the loosened dirt.

I wanted to dig the deep holes
that hold the long green poles
where all the playground parts connect.

When the poles are all in place,
they look like skinny trees,
but it's going to be my wild rain forest!

When I drew my dream playground,
I made a jungle gym with a monkey bar —
with real monkeys! and swinging vines! —
so we can leap in the canopy
and tightrope-walk among the trees
and boomerang with green bananas
and only come inside if it starts raining hard.

When you draw **your** playground,
will you spring between
high-rises like a superhero?
Are you the firefighter on the
swaying ladder who saves the day?
Is that you on the trapeze, high above
the crowd, hanging upside down?

We drew and we dreamed of a slide at our playground . . .
    and the factory made it for real! A triple slide!
        First an engineer designed it on a computer,
           a model with all the measurements just right.

A mold made of steel was cast,
    and barrels of plastic beads were poured into that empty shape.
        They melted. They cooled. And then—
           out popped our purple triple slide!

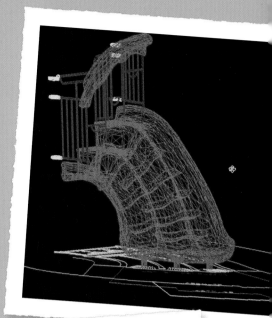

We drew and we dreamed of a climbing wall, too.
    And the factory designed it, built a model,
        cast a mold, melted the beads, and then—
           out popped a rocky block
               with stepping nooks and grabbing blocks
                   and a crater that leads into another world!

And our monkey bars—they built that dream with steel!
    With a white-hot torch, the workers bent the steel
        and melted metal to weld the pieces
           together so they'll never break apart.

For our playground . . . another truck delivered our slide, climbing wall, teeter-totter, swings, ladders, and all the rest. Everything arrived in pieces that had to be assembled. All together, our playground weighed over 5,000 pounds! That's like me and 125 friends!

When we built our playground,
   214 volunteers gathered at sunrise
      in the parking lot beside the empty space.

Parents, neighbors, teachers, grandparents,
   and so many people we didn't even know
      joined in to build our playground.

For six hours in the sweltering sun,
   they scooped up mulch and hauled it with tarps.
      They sawed and hammered lumber
         into benches and tables and flower boxes.

Nails, nuts and bolts, screws —
   they pounded, tightened, twisted, and drilled.

For our playground . . . the mulch that the truck brought was special mulch. It's chipped-up trees but with no leaves or bark, in pieces bigger than half an inch but smaller than an inch. When the chips pile together, they create a spongy surface. So when you run or jump or fall, you have a softer landing.

More mulch over here!
    Mix up another wheelbarrow of cement.
        It's not even nine a.m. — I'm already soaked with sweat!

We need another team to help us carry this!
    Who's got the level? Does that pole look straight?
        Careful, that paint's still wet!
            Behind you . . . coming through!

Our playground needed to be safe and sturdy and strong.
The slide, the monkey bars, the climbing wall —
every single piece — had to be anchored
deep into the ground with cement.

You should have seen the team of wheelbarrows!
They filled with sack after sack of cement.

Shovels split open each bag with a poof of dust.
Hoses splashed into the crumbly powder.
Slap! Scrape! Slosh! The shovels slapped and scooped
the slushy mixture into a muddy slop.

Sometimes it took two people to heave
the heavy wheelbarrow across the bumpy mulch
toward a post sunk in one of the fifty holes.
(Our playground was the moon . . .
those holes were its craters!)

When a wheelbarrow lifted, the slurry of cement
flopped into a hole. (They're two feet deep!
If I had jumped in one, only my shoulders and head
would poke above the ground.)

What is **cement**? It's crushed limestone that's blended with other materials, then heated. These marble-size chunks are ground up with another mineral, gypsum, that's soft and chalky. When water is added to this dry mix, it creates a thick slurry that first heats up and then cools into a very strong solid known as concrete.

Our playground's almost done!

Now the teams are tightening all the fasteners and braces
    so nothing will slip or jiggle on the posts.

And look! Look at all the strong people they need
    to heave the heavy slide above their heads . . .
        and then lower it — slowly, carefully —
        where it fits into the playground.
    Time to level it. Time to lock it into position.
        Don't you need someone to test it? I can!
    Not yet. Not now.

Almost done!
    Someone's digging holes for flowers
        in the just-now-finished planters.

Someone's smoothing out the ground
    between the tiles we got to paint.

Someone's cheering, *"Almost done! Great job!"*

How long would it take you—just
you—to build our playground?
The 214 volunteers, working
6 hours each, put in 1,284 hours.
If you worked 8 hours every day,
you'd be finished in 160 days.
That's nearly half a year! And
that's forgetting that so many
things require teamwork!

Opening day! We built a playground
   where we had no place to play before.

I'm the one sliding down the dinosaur,
   slipping straight across his back
      and swooping onto the mulch
         for a moonwalk back to the top.

I'm climbing Mount Everest!
   Trekking up the steep path
      and slithering among the caves.

We're all swinging through the jungle
   with the monkeys in the trees,
      snatching up coconuts that we'll juggle upside down
         or bowl across the ground.

Opening day — *KaBOOM!* — we did it!
We built a playground in our neighborhood!
How did we build it? *KaBOOM!*
How can you build yours? *KaBOOM!*

Ready to imagine your very own playground?
Grab a sheet of paper and let's go!

Pretend that your ideas are like you and your friends bursting outside for recess. Each one can go in a different direction. Each idea can be a different activity. On your paper, draw little pictures to keep track of what you dream up. Or have a grown-up help you write them down.

Instead of simply naming your favorite playground equipment, let your imagination run wild first! That way, a slide isn't just a slide. It's the chute that leads to the vault of a time machine. And a swing isn't just a swing. It's Pegasus, the horse with wings you ride across the galaxy!

Then picture somewhere — anywhere on Earth — where you'd like to play. Are you . . . *on a ship breaking through the Arctic ice? In an underground maze? Snorkeling with sea turtles in Australia?*

Now, if you could invite anyone in the world to play with you, who would it be? *The mermaid queen? A championship wrestler? A genie?* And who might *you* pretend to be?

Choose some actions, too. What game, sport, dance, or story might you enjoy in your dreamed-up place? *Is your lookout post atop an elephant, a lighthouse, or a satellite? Are you leaping over racetrack hurdles or open-mouthed alligators in a moat?*

Once you have lots of ideas, pick your favorite ones. Then see which pieces of playground equipment might capture what you've imagined. Change them, combine them, and arrange them in any way that best fulfills your dreamed-up playground.

Author's Note

The playground chronicled in this book is just one of the more than 2,200 KaBOOM! has helped to create. It was built in the summer of 2011 on the grounds of Andrew Academy, a charter school in Indianapolis, Indiana. Prior to this playground's construction, the available play areas for the students and neighborhood kids consisted of an empty field, a parking lot painted with faded Four Square and kickball lines, and a cluster of ancient, tubular-metal climbing structures. (One of the volunteers, a grandmother, told us, "I mean, those were here when *I* was a student.")

Teams from KaBOOM! and the sponsoring partner, PNC, joined the parents and staff of the school to create this safe, modern, welcoming playspace in their neighborhood. Along with photographers Ellen Kelson and Jennifer Cecil, I traveled there to document the creation of this playground.

As I hope this book makes clear, "the build" was not simply the construction of the equipment or the preparation of the site. It included the weeks and weeks of planning by dozens of community members and parents assembled into vital, invested committees. It included the efforts of